Discipling in Community

Transforming Small Groups
into
Discipling Communities

Alan Wagner

Discipling in Community

© Copyright Alan Wagner, 2015

143 Acutt Avenue, Rosehill, 4051 South Africa

alankwagner@gmail.com

ISBN: 978-0-620-64644-4

Cover design:	Alan and Niki Wagner
	Concept from www.openclipart.org
Editorial assistance:	Mark Krause and Niki Wagner

CONTENTS

Introduction: Why Are We Doing This?

I've been involved with church small groups for many years – as a member, as a leader and as an overseer of small group leaders. I *love* small groups! This is where we get to experience authentic community! This is where we can "drop our guard" and ask our awkward questions! This is where we can be vulnerable about our struggles with people who know us, love us, pray for us and believe in us! This is where we can take tentative "first steps" of faith that will later impact others outside of the group!

A church leader once remarked that one of the greatest miracles of church is that "people show up every Sunday" – even though they don't have to! If that is true, then it's probably an even greater miracle that people attend midweek small group meetings!

So why do we?

There are many positive reasons to do so, but there are also some unhelpful reasons – such as routine (we've always done this), compulsion (we feel obliged to go) and duty (we carry some responsibility for the group). I have observed that groups can continue for years, with many of the members attending reasonably regularly, driven only by routine, compulsion and duty. Such meetings may be pleasant, but they typically fall short of their potential to be life-changing groups that have a powerful impact on both their members and their community.

About a year ago, I began to re-examine two vital aspects of church life: *discipleship* and *community*. This involved reading many articles, blogs and books and having conversations with leaders who were making significant advances in these arenas. The contents of this book are a result of this process – an amalgamation of the wisdom and experience of many.

This book is not "a book of answers" – in fact, it asks many questions! The goal is to help you to re-examine discipleship and community for yourself, and then to start a journey of discipling in community in your small group.

REDISCOVERING DISCIPLESHIP

Then the eleven disciples went to Galilee, to the mountain where Jesus had told them to go. When they saw him, they worshiped him; but some doubted. Then Jesus came to them and said, "All authority in heaven and on earth has been given to me. Therefore go and make disciples of all nations, baptizing them inn the name of the Father and of the Son and of the Holy Spirit, and teaching them to obey everything I have commanded you. And surely I am with you always, to the very end of the age."

- Matthew 28:16-20 (NIV)

1: Christian vs Disciple

The disciples were called Christians first at Antioch.

- Acts 11:26 (NIV)

Do the words matter?

What does it mean to be a "Christian"? In the twenty-first century, the word now means very different things to different people. Here are some definitions I found during a quick internet browse:

- "A believer in Christianity."

- "One who professes belief in the teachings of Jesus Christ."

- "Following the religion based on the life and teachings of Jesus."

- "One who professes belief in Jesus as Christ."

 - "A person who has received Christian baptism."

Professing to be a "Christian" can therefore mean a great deal – but it can also mean very little. This explains why people who call themselves "Christians" can have very different opinions and live very different lifestyles. It all depends on what the word "Christian" means to them!

A study of the word "Christian(s)" in the Bible reveals that it originated from outside of the church (Acts 11:26) – members of the early church generally called themselves *disciples*. The word "Christian(s)" is only found three times in the Bible.

In contrast, the word "disciple(s)" is found 285 times (counted in the 1984 NIV). Jesus called people to be his *disciples*, and his "Great Commission" to his disciples was to:

"...go and make disciples of all nations..."

- Matthew 28:19 (NIV)

The word "disciple" was well understood by the early church. The Greek word "mathetes" means a "learner" or "apprentice". It implied devotion, because a disciple:

- followed their master,

- learned from their teaching and

- imitated their lifestyle.

Jesus made it very clear that being his disciple required the utmost devotion; consider this radical call:

> *"If anyone comes to me and does not hate his father and mother, his wife and children, his brothers and sisters--yes, even his own life--he cannot be my disciple. And anyone who does not carry his cross and follow me cannot be my disciple... any of you who does not give up everything he has cannot be my disciple."*

> – Luke 14:26, 27, 33 (NIV)

We could therefore define a "disciple" as:

"a devoted follower who learns from, and imitates, their master".

If we call ourselves "Christians", it may not mean that much; if we call ourselves "disciples of Christ", that means a great deal!

Disciples making disciples

The variant of the Greek word that is used in the Great Commission – translated "make disciples" ("matheteuo") – tells us more, because it has a two-fold meaning:

(1) to *be* a disciple, and

(2) to *make* disciples.

Jesus' commission adds a second dimension to discipleship. To be a disciple of Jesus implies that we will also become "disciplers" – people who "make disciples" of Jesus.

A great picture of "disciples making disciples" can be seen in Paul's second letter to Timothy:

*And the things you have heard **me** say in the presence of many witnesses entrust to **reliable people** who will also be qualified to teach **others**.*

- 2 Timothy 2:2 (NIV)

Notice the pattern of *disciples making disciples*:

- Paul discipled Timothy.

   - Timothy was to disciple "reliable people".

      - The "reliable people" would, in turn, disciple "others".

Discipleship is therefore much more than a "personal experience"; it is a lifestyle that impacts the lives of others. Disciples make disciples.

Exponential growth

Many have wondered how the church grew from about 120 people in an upper room to more than 50% of the Roman Empire in about 250 years. Preaching at meetings can bring about a steady increase, but disciples making disciples brings about *exponential* growth. Consider the following example:

If *one* disciple makes *five* disciples;

  5 disciples make 25 disciples;

    25 disciples make 125 disciples;

      125 disciples make 625 disciples;

        625 disciples make 3 125 disciples;

          3 125 disciples make 15 625 disciples;

            15 625 disciples make 78 125 disciples...

If each disciple made *ten* disciples, the last number would be *ten million* disciples!

Evangelist Billy Graham was asked, "If you were a pastor of a large church in a principal city, what would be your plan of action?" His answer surprised many:

"I think one of the first things I would do would be to a get a small group of eight or ten or twelve people around me that would meet a few hours a week and pay the price!

"It would cost them something in time and effort. I would share with them everything I have, over a period of years. Then I would actually have twelve ministers among the lay people who in turn could take eight or ten or twelve more and teach them. I know one or two churches that are doing that, and it is revolutionizing the church.

"Christ, I think, set the pattern. He spent most of his time with twelve men. He didn't spend it with a great crowd. In fact, every time he had a great crowd it seems to me that there weren't too many results. The great results, it seems to me, came in this personal interview and in the time he spent with his twelve."

(Source: The Master Plan of Evangelism" by Robert E. Coleman.)

Discipleship may appear to have a small impact at first, as we disciple a relatively small number of people. But as *those* disciples make disciples – and as *their* disciples make disciples, the impact is one that grows *exponentially*. As such, discipleship is profoundly "evangelistic"!

When we realise the immense impact of disciples who make disciples, we will surely seek to become one – and to make some!

Disciples of *WHO*?

When we speak of "disciples making disciples", we could fall into a dangerous trap – that of making "our own" disciples who follow *us*. This is very dangerous territory! This is how groups can grow that follow one influential – but imperfect – person, instead of Jesus. This is how divisions can grow, heresies can spread and cults can form.

Paul had to rebuke the new church at Corinth for becoming "disciples of men":

My brothers, some from Chloe's household have informed me that there are quarrels among you. What I mean is this: One of you says, "I follow Paul"; another, "I follow Apollos"; another, "I follow Cephas [Peter]"; still another, "I follow Christ."

Is Christ divided? Was Paul crucified for you? Were you baptized into the name of Paul?

> - 1 Corinthians 1:11-13 (NIV)

As we seek to make disciples, it is crucial that we make disciples of *Christ*, not disciples of ourselves. People have discipled me, but I must be a disciple of *Christ*. As I strive to "make disciples" of others, I strive to make them disciples of *Christ*. *Christ* is the head of the Church. *Christ* is the master we are devoted to. When we make disciples of Christ, *he* is the focus, not any discipler. This keeps us united and this helps our message stay pure.

This correct focus also keeps us "spiritually alive" and spiritually empowered. Jesus is our source of life – we need to draw on *his* life, not on that of our leaders or disciplers! Jesus made it very clear that he is the source of the spiritual life we need:

I am the vine; you are the branches. If you remain in me and I in you, you will bear much fruit; apart from me you can do nothing. If you do not remain in me, you are like a branch that is thrown away and withers; such branches are picked up, thrown into the fire and burned.

If you remain in me and my words remain in you, ask whatever you wish, and it will be done for you. This is to my Father's glory, that you bear much fruit, showing yourselves to be my disciples.

> - John 15:5-8 (NIV)

Some of us have seen the opposite of this in small groups. We have seen people cling to, and draw on, their leader instead of Jesus. As explained by Jesus, this does not work – the leader is unable to provide the life that their people need. So the members get disappointed and frustrated, as their needs remain unmet; and the leaders get exhausted and frustrated as they are unable to meet the members' demands!

It is therefore vital that we ensure that our discipleship efforts are focussed on growing everyone as *disciples of Christ*.

As we commence our journey of "discipling in community", we must understand what it really means to be a disciple of Christ:

- A disciple of Christ is *devoted follower of Christ*, who *learns* from him, and *imitates* him.

- A disciple of Christ obeys the commission of Christ to "make disciples of all nations". *Disciples make disciples.*

- A disciple of Christ has an *impact on their greater community* because of their Christ-like behaviour. Their impact may seem small at first (making a relatively small number of disciples), but it is actually *exponential* in its impact as all of those disciples make disciples.

- A disciple of Christ is first-and-foremost *devoted to Jesus*, not their leader or discipler.

- A disciple of Christ learns to *draw on Jesus* for their spiritual vitality, not their leader or discipler.

As we grasp these truths and begin to live them out, our lives will be transformed.

As we learn to do this *together*, our small groups will be transformed!

As our lives and our small groups are transformed, we will impact those around us – our *communities* can be transformed!

2: Knowledge vs Life

My first small group experience was in the early 1980s. It was called a "Bible Study", but it was really a group of (largely new) believers sharing Bible verses that had either inspired them or confused them. We read, debated and asked our oldest member to please help us!

Later, I discovered that there were many "serious" (more formal) Bible study groups who followed structured programs of learning from the Bible. As one with a teaching gift, I found this very appealing! When I was given the opportunity to lead a small group, Bible teaching was certainly my main objective! Over the years, however, I have learned that small groups need to do far more than study together if we want to grow as disciples. Sadly, it is possible to grow in *knowledge* without growing in *maturity* or *impact*!

When we read about the Garden of Eden in Genesis, we read that there were two trees in the centre: the tree of *life* and the tree of the *knowledge* of good and evil. When we read about the Holy City in Revelation, we read that only the tree of *life* is there:

Now the LORD God had planted a garden in the east, in Eden; and there he put the man he had formed. And the LORD God made all kinds of trees grow out of the ground--trees that were pleasing to the eye and good for food. In the middle of the garden were the tree of life and the tree of the knowledge of good and evil.

- Genesis 2:8-9 (NIV)

Then the angel showed me the river of the water of life, as clear as crystal, flowing from the throne of God and of the Lamb down the middle of the great street of the city. On each side of the river stood the tree of life, bearing twelve crops of fruit, yielding its fruit every month. And the leaves of the tree are for the healing of the nations.

- Revelation 22:1-2 (NIV)

I don't want to develop a "doctrine" around this, but I do believe that this is significant. The tree of *life* is the tree that we need! Pursuing knowledge can be a very noble cause, but it is not the *most* noble – seeking the *life of God* is the greater goal!

Jesus rebuked the Pharisees for this error:

> *"You diligently study the Scriptures because you think that by them you possess eternal life. These are the Scriptures that testify about me, yet you refuse to come to me to have life."*

- John 5:39-40 (NIV)

Jesus' rebuke was not for diligently studying the Scriptures; it was for thinking that their diligent study would secure them eternal life. But eternal life is not *knowing <u>about</u> God* – it is *<u>knowing</u> God*:

> *"Now this is eternal life: that they may know you, the only true God, and Jesus Christ, whom you have sent."*

- John 17:3 (NIV)

The Pharisees were diligent students of the Scriptures – the very words that point to Jesus as the source of life. But they failed to look through the lens of the Scriptures to recognise Jesus as their saviour. They grew in knowledge, but failed to come to Jesus for life.

As we seek to become better disciples of Christ, we will find studying the Bible – particularly the Gospels – very helpful. But remember, the objective is not to just grow in *knowledge*. The objective is to learn Jesus' words and ways so that we can get to know *him* better – to grow in our *relationship* with him!

3: The Dimensions of Discipleship

The life of discipleship is a rich, multi-faceted one. As discipleship becomes our lifestyle, our life gets bigger and richer; it is an exciting, rewarding adventure!

There are many aspects to the life of discipleship, but we can picture it as having three primary "dimensions":

"UP"   - loving God

"IN"   - loving one another

"OUT" - loving the lost

UP: Loving God

Therefore, I urge you, brothers, in view of God's mercy, to offer your bodies as living sacrifices, holy and pleasing to God – this is your spiritual [or reasonable] act of worship.

- Romans 12:1 (NIV)

We are first-and-foremost disciples of Jesus. We must therefore be firstly – and above all else – devoted to Jesus. He is our Saviour. He is our Lord. He is our source of life. He is our first priority.

Paul urged the disciples in Rome to respond to the incredible mercy of God in Jesus by devoting themselves to him. This is a totally appropriate response: *he died for us, so we live for him.*

When some of us think about worship, we think about singing or about church meetings. Paul wrote about worship in a far broader sense; *we worship God with our whole life.* He presented worship as an offering of a *living* sacrifice instead of a dead one – of our lives fully yielded to God.

Eugene Peterson paraphrased Romans 12:1 like this in "The Message":

So here's what I want you to do, God helping you: Take your everyday, ordinary life – your sleeping, eating, going-to-work, and walking-around life – and place it before God as an offering. Embracing what God does for you is the best thing you can do for him.

He continues this paraphrase of verse 2:

Don't become so well-adjusted to your culture that you fit into it without even thinking. Instead, fix your attention on God. You'll be changed from the inside out. Readily recognize what he wants from you, and quickly respond to it. Unlike the culture around you, always dragging you down to its level of immaturity, God brings the best out of you, develops well-formed maturity in you.

Discipleship starts with us surrendering completely to Christ.

It continues as we live in a deepening relationship with him.

Its outworking is transformation – as Jesus leads us into his ways, our lives are transformed!

IN: Loving one another

"A new command I give you: Love one another. As I have loved you, so you must love one another. By this all men will know that you are my disciples, if you love one another."

- John 13:34-35 (NIV)

Jesus told his disciples to live as a *community*. This was not a suggestion; it was a command. This community was to be based on a love for one another – a love that was so strong that it could be likened to Jesus' love. *This depth of love would be the proof to the world that they were true disciples of Jesus.*

This kind of community is a beautiful thing, full of the life of God. The early church described in Acts lived as this kind of community:

All the believers were together and had everything in common. Selling their possessions and goods, they gave to anyone as he had need. Every day they continued to meet together in the temple courts. They broke bread in their homes and ate together with glad and sincere hearts, praising God and enjoying the favour of all the people. And the Lord added to their number daily those who were being saved.

- Acts 2:44-47 (NIV)

They were "all together". They "had everything in common". They sold personal possessions to help others who were in need. They met regularly in public and in each other's homes. Outsiders saw something magnificent and compelling in this community – and came to faith in Jesus as a result!

Listen to the cry of Jesus' heart as he prayed for us before going to the cross:

> *"I am praying not only for these disciples but also for all who will ever believe in me through their message. I pray that they will all be one, just as you and I are one—as you are in me, Father, and I am in you. And may they be in us so that the world will believe you sent me.*
>
> *"I have given them the glory you gave me, so they may be one as we are one. I am in them and you are in me. May they experience such perfect unity that the world will know that you sent me and that you love them as much as you love me."*

- John 17:20-23 (NLT)

Jesus prayed that all who would come to believe in him would enjoy an experience of unity in community that is best described as being "one". He prayed for such a magnificent unity that those who saw it would believe that God loves *them* and sent Jesus to save them!

This prayer includes us! O that this cry of the heart of Jesus would stir us to pursue greater unity in the family of God and in our small groups! O for a vision of a community that is so magnificent that it convinces those who have yet to believe in Jesus that he *is* Saviour!

OUT: Loving the lost

> *"All authority in heaven and on earth has been given to me.*
> *Therefore **go and make disciples of all nations**, baptizing them inn the name of the Father and of the Son and of the Holy Spirit, and teaching them to obey everything I have commanded you. And surely I am with you always, to the very end of the age."*

- Matthew 28:18-20 (NIV)

Some have been taught that "mission" is something for "hard-core" disciples. "Mission" is seen as a courageous person or family going to some foreign, forsaken or hostile territory. But this is only one aspect of mission. As disciples of Jesus, we *all* have a mission – to make disciples of all nations. Wherever we are, (studying, working, playing etc.) we are to make disciples. If he sends us elsewhere, then we go to our *next* mission field!

Many of us have been taught that discipleship is for "believers only" – for the "converted". But Jesus' disciples were not "believers" when he first called them; they grew in their faith as he discipled them! Even at the end of Matthew's gospel, just before the "Great Commission", we find this surprising statement:

> *Then the eleven disciples went to Galilee, to the mountain where Jesus had told them to go. When they saw him, they worshiped him;* ***but some doubted.***

> - Matthew 28:16-17 (NIV)

When we broaden our view of discipleship like this, we "evangelise" differently. Our commission or mission is to make disciples, coming alongside people and helping them on their faith-journey – wherever they may be on that journey. So our first conversation does not have to be a Gospel presentation; it could be an invitation to coffee, dinner, a movie or a sports event! Discipleship takes time and is built on relationship; so our first steps should be to build relationship. This is far less intimidating, and paves the way to true discipleship. As people get to know us, they will soon discover that we are rather different (if we are living like Jesus) – and those differences will open the way to pointing them to Jesus.

Discipleship is truly a rich, multi-faceted life! It begins with us becoming *disciples of Jesus*. It is sustained by a growing *relationship with Jesus*. It is best experienced and expressed with other disciples – in *community*. And it has a positive impact on others as we become *disciple-makers*, and reach out to our greater community.

These are truly glorious goals to pursue!

4: The Journey of Discipleship

When we examine the Gospels, we can see that the disciples "walked a journey of faith" over several years:

Jesus called them to be his disciples...

    As they followed him, their faith grew...

        They put their faith in him as Saviour and served him as Lord...

           They then went out and made disciples!

The goal to transform our small groups into discipling communities is a godly and a noble one, but we need to know that it is a *journey*, not a single step. Each member will experience times when they need to make key personal decisions and overcome significant personal obstacles. If we are unaware that there is a progression that must unfold, we could try to "force the end result". We could become "legalistic" and "moralistic", focussing on keeping rules and "behaving the right way" instead of helping people to walk their own road of discipleship.

The journey of discipleship can be thought of as a progression through four phases:

- "Unbelievers" (still to be fully convinced that Jesus is Saviour)
- "Believers" (convinced that Jesus is Saviour; life committed into his hands)
- "Disciples" (devoted followers of Jesus)
- "Disciplers" (disciples who are making disciples)

This is not presented as a "definitive process to follow", or as a "list of levels to achieve", but as a way of recognising that there is a progressive nature to the discipleship journey. Some people hear the Gospel, come to faith and almost immediately begin life as "disciples who make disciples". Others spend a lot of time in one "phase".

For example, some struggle for a long time to be fully convinced about Jesus. For others, the decision to become a devoted follower of Jesus has major implications (e.g. making significant lifestyle changes, abandoning the faith of their family or facing persecution). We must understand that each person has their own "faith journey" to walk.

Discipling entails walking alongside them "where they are at" and helping them to take their next steps.

"Situational Discipleship"

Because the journey of discipleship has a progressive nature, disciplers need to recognise "where a disciple is at" and help them in a way that is both appropriate and helpful. Here are some suggested "helpful approaches" based on the phases already described:

"Unbelievers":

Don't expect them to come to you; go to them.

Approach them as equals – you are not "better than them". You are an "object of mercy" and a "work in progress"!

Recognise that aspects of our faith and lifestyle are weird to many unbelievers. Try to make them "comfortably uncomfortable", not compromising on the truth, but being realistic about where they are. For example, you may find their language foul, but they probably regard it as normal. You may have no problem believing the Bible is God's word, but they may well see it as just another religious book.

Avoid "Christianese" (words that Christians understand but others don't) – such foreign language alienates people.

Remember that relationship is foundational to discipleship – so build the relationship and seek to be a blessing to them. Someone said, "They don't care how much you know until they know how much you care." Listen to their objections and questions with the motive of seeking to *understand* where they are, rather than giving them the right answer.

"Believers":

Believers have crossed the most important line of faith, but they still have a journey ahead. Don't assume that they have been instantly transformed into "model disciples" – and don't demand that of them!

"Life-on-life" personal relationships are invaluable to help new believers to move forward. Many will not ask their "big questions" or share their "big struggles" in a public setting; they will wait for a private conversation.

It may surprise you that all believers do not have the same understanding of the Gospel – it depends on how the Gospel was presented to them. We therefore need to make sure that new believers understand the Gospel, the call to discipleship and the Great Commission. This is where solid foundational teaching is really valuable; we want to build on a solid foundation!

"Disciples":

Because disciples are actively seeking and following Jesus, their needs are different. Disciples typically need to be *equipped* and *encouraged:* firstly in their personal journey of discipleship, and secondly as they get on with their own mission – to make disciples. We need to help disciples to "find their mission fields" and encourage them as they take first steps towards making disciples.

"Disciplers":

Disciplers primarily need to be *encouraged*, as the work of discipling can be challenging! Discipling some people is easy; other people face serious challenges and walking with them requires patience, persistence and much prayer!

Changing your small group leadership style

If you are in a more traditional type of small group, you are quite possibly operating as a *leader*, *teacher* and *carer*. This mode of operation makes for "nice" groups, but it is easy for people to be passive in this environment – just "coming to the meeting" and maybe participating in some small way.

A helpful shift from this mode is to shift to *"facilitator"*. This means that you do less things yourself and instead help others to do them. Practically, this can be as simple as making rosters so that members can take turns to do different things.

A very helpful leadership shift is to move away from the traditional "teacher" role. Many people love teaching (not as much as the teachers do!), but we want to help people move from "knowledge to life". We also want to dismantle barriers that keep people from leading their own small groups – and one major barrier is the "I can't teach well enough" barrier. Instead of having "teaching" in the small group time (this is usually happening on Sunday already), shift the focus to testimonies and to real-life challenges that the members are facing that need prayer. Some great questions to ask the group are: "What did God say to you this week? How did you recognise him speaking? What did you do about it? What did God do?" One or two responses are likely to open up a healthy, helpful conversation that builds everyone up as disciples.

In the end, small group leaders need to operate more and more as "guides" and "shepherds". Our goal is to make our small groups "high growth environments" where disciples encourage one another to continue moving forward on their discipleship path.

REDISCOVERING COMMUNITY

They devoted themselves to the apostles' teaching and to the **fellowship***, *to the* breaking *of bread and to prayer. Everyone was filled with awe, and many wonders and miraculous signs were done by the apostles.* **All** *the believers were* **together** *and had* **everything in common.** *Selling their possessions and goods, they gave to anyone as he had need. Every day they* **continued to meet together** *in the* **temple courts**. *They broke bread in their* **homes** *and ate together with glad and sincere hearts, praising God and enjoying the* **favour of all the people.** *And* **the Lord added to their number daily** *those who were being saved.*

- Acts 2:42-47 (NIV)

* *koinōnia (koy-nohn-ee'-ah): partnership, participation, social intercourse, monetary benefaction, contribution, distribution, fellowship.*

- Strong's Dictionary

5: Meetings vs Community

Meeting together is a Biblical value. The early church was known for regularly meeting together, both on a large scale in public gatherings and on a small scale in homes (Acts 2:42, 46). We are urged not to give up meeting together, even though some do (Hebrews 10:25). Meeting together is a good thing!

That said, we must beware of falling into the trap of simply "meeting for the meeting's sake". Attending the meeting can become the goal, something that we tick off on our checklist of "right things to do". If that happens, we can think that we're doing well just because meeting attendance is reasonably consistent. When meeting attendance becomes the objective, we can lose sight of *why* we meet, and our meetings can lose some of their potential impact. It is sadly possible to have a small group that meets consistently, yet has very little impact on its members or on "outsiders".

In chapter three (Dimensions of Discipleship), we identified the dimension of *community*. Acts 2:42-47 gives a picture of community that may be radically different from your small group experience:

- They were "devoted" to fellowship.

- They had "everything in common"; those "with" sold personal possessions to help others who were "without".

- They met in public and in homes.

- They enjoyed the favour of the greater community.

- Their community had such a positive and powerful impact that there was a constant stream of conversions.

It is tempting to dismiss some aspects of this New Testament community as peculiar to the culture of the day – surely we can't do that in our day and in our situation? I propose that we take a different view: instead of seeing this as *daunting*, let's see this as *inspiring!* Let's allow this picture of community inspire us to reach out a little further and enjoy more than we presently do!

Jesus' "new command" sets the tone for community as his disciples:

"So now I am giving you a new commandment:

Love each other. Just as I have loved you, you should love each other.

Your love for one another will prove to the world that you are my disciples."

- John 13:34-35 (NLT)

"My command is this: Love each other as I have loved you. Greater love has no one than this, that he lay down his life for his friends."

- John 15:12-13 (NIV)

Jesus commands us as his disciples to love one another in the same way that he loves us – by laying our lives down for each other. This is a level of relationship that goes far deeper than regular meeting attendance! We are to share our very lives with one another!

We now have three compelling reasons for community:

1. Jesus commands it.

For some of us, this is all we need to hear; Jesus commands us to love one another as he loves us! He is our Lord and we are his disciples; if this is his command, then this is what we must do!

2. It is good for us.

From the Acts 2 description of community and Jesus' new command, we see community as something that has a *common good*. We all help each other. Those who are strong help those who are weak. Those who are rich help those who are poor. The end response from within the community of disciples was to praise God – *this was a good experience!*

3. It reaches the lost.

Those in the greater community who had yet to believe were truly impressed by what they saw (there was favour) – and there was a steady stream of new converts. This comes as no surprise; Jesus said that the depth of his disciples' love would convince others that this is something truly authentic – this is the "real deal"!

A healthy small group is a wonderful way to experience life in community. But it takes more than just attending a weekly meeting! If we are to enjoy community, we are going to have to invest in building relationships, getting to *really* know one another. We are going to have to build *trust*, so that we can be honest and vulnerable with each other.

For example, if I am in financial need, I need to admit this to my group for them to help. If my marriage or my business is in trouble, I need to admit this to the group for them to help. If I don't feel safe with them though, I will be reluctant to be this vulnerable. If the group is just a *meeting*, I will probably struggle on silently. If the group is a *community*, I will share my struggles, knowing that my "small group family" want to help me.

Many "Sunday conversations" are superficial:

"Hello, how are you?"

"Fine – and you?"

"Great! Enjoy the meeting! / Have a great week!"

Practically speaking, there is often little time for a significant conversation in these contexts; the meeting is about to start or we are heading out somewhere. Our best efforts are likely to be hurried – that is why we need better opportunities to engage. Small group gatherings are one time when we can connect at a deeper level.

Building relationships and building trust takes time and effort. We cannot simply "instruct" our people to know each other and trust each other. What we can do is create an *environment* and organise *activities* that *make it easier* for the group to grow into a community. We need to allow our meetings to get "messy" and change our plans when people need to talk and ask questions. We need to intentionally make time for people to "just connect" with each other.

The appendices "Five Levels of Communication" and "The Johari Window" may help you to better appreciate and understand what we want to achieve:

-   We want to help our people to "move to the next level" in their communication. If they are at level one and two, help them to move to level three (don't expect them to jump straight to five!). For example, instead of teaching, present a question and ask leading questions that prompt people to share their views.

- We want our people to "know each other and be known to each other". We want them to tell us more about themselves. We want them to learn more about themselves.

Back to "the meeting"...

As we seek to build community, view your small group meeting as the *foundation* upon which you will build community. A group of people who meet together regularly is a wonderful thing – it is the beginning of a community! It is not the end goal, but a starting point to build something truly magnificent!

6: Inward vs Outward

"My prayer is not for them alone. I pray also for those who will believe in me through their message, that all of them may be one, Father, just as you are in me and I am in you. May they also be in us so that the world may believe that you have sent me."

- John 17:20-21 (NIV)

As Jesus prayed for his disciples, notice that his prayers had an "outward progression":

He prayed for his disciples...

then he prayed for the disciples that his disciples would make...

then he prayed for the world.

Notice too that this "outwardly progressing prayer" was actually a prayer for unity! Jesus was praying that we would be one – united in community – *"so that the world may believe"*!

Some people think that community and mission/evangelism are two different goals – even opposing goals. To some, community is "inward" and mission is "outward". There are valid reasons for this thinking: some small groups are totally focussed on themselves as a community and have no interest in "those out there". Others are "so spiritually minded that they are no earthly good", having glorious times together, but being totally irrelevant in their greater communities.

Jesus presents community as "missional"!

When we live in a healthy, visible community, this demonstrates to others that the Gospel is true – that the Father so loved the world that he sent the Son to save it. Community that is lived out God's way is not opposed to mission; it is missional!

Looking at this another way, when we work on building community, we work on building "a culture that includes" – one of acceptance and belonging. This same culture that helps our members engage also draws "outsiders" in. It is a welcoming, inviting culture – we want to include *others* in our lives too!

Peter presents "community with impact" in his first letter:

But you are a chosen PEOPLE, a royal PRIESTHOOD, a holy NATION, God's special possession, THAT YOU may declare the praises of him who called you out of darkness into his wonderful light. Once you were not a people, but now you are the people of God; once you had not received mercy, but now you have received mercy.

Dear friends, I urge you, as foreigners and exiles, to abstain from sinful desires, which wage WAR against your soul. Live such good LIVES AMONG the pagans that, though they accuse you of doing wrong, they may SEE your good DEEDS and GLORIFY God on the day he visits us.

- 1 Peter 2:9-12 (NIV)

Corporate Identity:

Notice that Peter presents a "corporate identity" to us: as a community we are a *people*, a *priesthood*, a *nation*, God's *special possession*. As a community, we have a profound identity together!

Positioned to Influence:

Peter positions us "among the pagans". We are not supposed to be *removed* from the greater community where we live; we are supposed to be *amongst* them! Our community needs to be "engaged" in the world around us! (Some small groups choose to meet in restaurants or coffee shops for this reason.)

Active to Influence:

Peter then writes of some of the things that we *do*. As we live in community "among the pagans", we do "good deeds" that they see. We are not a "spiritual secret service"; we are a "spiritual public service"! Our counter-culture lifestyle may result in opposition (such as being accused of doing wrong), yet it also results in glory to God!

The Ultimate Goal of Community:

Although community brings tremendous benefits to its members, the ultimate goal of community is to impact the world so that they glorify God. The ultimate goal of our community is to be such a powerful demonstration of the love of God that unbelievers become disciples of Christ!

In his book "Community", Brad House writes:

"I endeavour to affirm community as a gift of God's grace for the purpose of exalting the Son and making him known. In other words, community is not about us; it is about God. Community is an instrument of worship, a weapon against sin, and a tool for evangelism – all for the exaltation of Jesus...

"We do not have community groups to close the back door of the church. We do not have groups because people need to belong or we need to care for one another. These are good but secondary effects of authentic community. These effects are not the foundation. We have community groups because we have seen the glory of God and we have been given the grace to live our lives to exalt the Christ. We have community groups because we have been reconciled to God and one another. We once were not a people but now we are a people of God's own possession. We have community groups as a proclamation of the goodness of our God and testimony to the completed work of the cross. This is the foundation for gospel-saturated community that will overflow with life."

REINVENTING YOUR SMALL GROUP

"Insanity: doing the same thing over and over again and expecting different results."

- Albert Einstein (attributed)

Rut - A settled and monotonous routine that is hard to escape.

- WordWeb Dictionary

7: Taking an Honest Look

If we want our small groups to become discipleship communities, we will need to do more than just *teach* our members about discipleship and community. We will need to *make changes* – changes in the way we live *individually* and in what we do as *groups*.

We can learn a great deal from those who have gone ahead of us in this arena. As we do so though, beware of seeking "the magic bullet" or the "formula for success". What works in one group may not work in yours. The bravest, most helpful first step will be to take an honest look – maybe a brutally honest look – at how you are *really* doing. When we know where we are, we are most likely to recognise the next step that we need to take.

Keith Meyer, in his book "Whole Life Transformation", recorded this "brutal confession":

> *"How did I get to the place where I was so off-task, caring more about my church's "organizational extension and survival" and measuring success in business terms – attendance, buildings and cash – rather than in becoming and making mature disciples of Jesus? How did church become more of a business organization for consumers of religious goods and services than a training ground of followers of Jesus?"*

Your small group may not be in this place – but you need to know what place they are in if you are to make the right changes.

As we evaluate how we are doing, we need to make sure we are looking at the right things. We are not looking at how "hip and happening" we are. We are not looking at our meeting format or lack thereof. We are not looking at our songs, our music, or our use of technology. We are looking at how well we are doing *as disciples of Jesus* – devoted followers who learn from him and imitate him. We are looking at how closely our *community* resembles the Biblical priorities of lives laid down in love for one another, of unity and of impact on the greater community.

In his article "Hanging Great Weight on Thin Wires", Neil Cole wrote:

"Your church is only as good as her disciples. A hot band, dynamic preaching, state-of-the-art facilities and wonderful programs do not make a great church if the disciples are simply consumers and unengaged in the grand work of making disciples. But if the disciples in your church are empowered and engaged in mission, than your church is strong and healthy, even if you do not have laser lights or fog machines."

Here are some questions we could ask ourselves as individuals and as communities. As we ask and answer them, we need to guard our hearts.

-   Watch out for *denial*, the desire to "give the right answer" instead of the truth.

-   Watch out for *defensiveness*, the desire to excuse what we find.

-   Watch out for *demoralisation*, the feeling that "we're too far off the mark to ever get there".

As you ask and answer the questions, think about *positive steps* you can take to move into a better place. Don't try to map the entire route, just look for the *first steps*.

Discipleship

- *Relationship with God*: are we growing in our relationship with the Father? Is our prayer life deepening? Are we getting better at hearing God? Is our love for him deepening?

- *Life of God*: is God supernaturally at work in us?

- *Character*: are we growing in Christ-like attributes such as love, grace, peace and humility?

- *Submission*: are we obeying the Scriptures? Are we making changes when we see differences between God's ways and ours?

- *World view*: are we seeing the world through the lens of the Kingdom of God or the lens of prevailing culture?

- *Reach*: how is our impact on others – are we making disciples yet?

Community

- *Foundation*: do we have the foundation of a small group who meet consistently? What factors hinder us from meeting consistently?

- *Health*: is our group *good* for the members? What aspects are helpful? What aspects are unhelpful? Am *I* good for the group? What do *I* need to change to be helpful to the group?

- *Impact*: is our small group visible to the greater community in any way? Who do we impact? Other than our group and our church leaders, who really cares if we exist?

- *Communication*: at what level are most of our conversations (see appendix on levels of communication)? Do we really know each other (see appendix on the Johari Window)? How can we "go deeper"?

- *Safety*: do members feel safe to be vulnerable in the group? Do confidential matters "leak" or do we guard each other's honour?

- *Integrity*: do we "walk the talk" (e.g. praying for one another when asked to, helping and encouraging one another)?

Culture

- *Consumerism*: Consumerism is an enemy of *discipleship*; it is focussed on our needs being met and opposed to sacrifices that don't promise personal benefit. Have you been lured into consumer thinking? Are you working through this cultural barrier to embrace sacrifice and putting Jesus and others ahead of you?

- *Individualism*: Individualism is an enemy of *community*. In some cultures, it is firmly entrenched – "my life is *my* life and none of your business". Have you been taught this? If so, are you working at breaking through your cultural barriers to embrace community?

- *Materialism*: Materialism is an enemy of *mission*. It seeks to gain, to own and to hold onto. It values this present life more than eternity. Mission is too costly for the materialist. Have you been taught materialism? If so, are you working at giving and releasing for the sake of others? Are you shifting focus from "earthly treasure" to "heavenly treasure"?

- *Entitlement*: Entitlement is an enemy of *sacrifice*. Have you been taught to "fight for your rights" – or that you "deserve" to be given certain things? Are your personal goals immovable? If so, are you working at "laying down your rights"?

There are many questions we could ask. Some of these may not be relevant to your group. These lists may be too long for your group (remember, we don't want to be overwhelmed, just challenged). You may think of some other questions that are more relevant to your group. The objective is to "take an honest look", to do some healthy "soul-searching", and to identify some things that need to be improved.

8: Exploring New Ways Together

Exploring new, better ways *together* is a tremendous way to build your community. Leaders, please lead the process, but don't dominate the conversations and don't feel that you have to come up with all the answers. Different people will see different needs and different solutions – and these conversations will help the members get to know each other and appreciate each other better.

Before you seek the answers though, make sure you all understand the questions! Work through the contents of this book individually and as a group so that you all have a good view of the goals – to grow as disciples and as a community. Answer the questions of the previous chapter individually and then as a group. [If you lead a church small group, you have the author's permission to print, photocopy and/or electronically distribute the contents of this book *for your small group members*.]

Dreaming together

Take time as individuals to dream and then share your responses over a few weeks:

- What could discipleship look like for *you*? Who could *you* disciple? Who could disciple *you*?

- What could discipleship look like for your *small group*?

- How can we "do community" better?

- Do we need to have different kinds of meetings at different times to achieve different goals? What do you see?

- How can we make our little community matter to the "greater community" of our neighbourhood/town/city?

Remember:

- Don't confine your dreaming to the "weekly meeting in a home" mentality. Think "out of the box".

- "One size doesn't fit all". Your group does not have to be the same as the other groups.

- Some ideas spark other ideas. Encourage members to share ideas even if they aren't sure "how good they are".

- Don't try to do everything every time you meet; rather do one or two things well each time you gather.

- Don't try to run too fast ("transform your group overnight"); focus on consistently moving in the right direction.

- Celebrate your successes, however small they may seem!

Exploring together

Experiment: Sometimes we find our way to what works by trying several different ideas. We don't know if that idea is a good one, but if we try it, we will – as someone put it, "if you don't go you won't know"!

Take "first steps": start "where you are" with "what you can see" of the way ahead!

Learn through success and failure: Don't be afraid to fail – if an idea doesn't work, you will still learn!

Adapt and advance: After you've tried something, evaluate how it went, think of possible improvements, and *give it an even better go!* Keep learning and keep advancing!

Breaking the "teaching mould"

A widely established ingredient of small group meetings is some sort of teaching. While teaching is valuable, chances are excellent that you are taught every week on Sunday. While many people love to be taught or to teach, insisting on teaching has some surprising negative effects:

- It imposes a big "entry requirement" for potential small group leaders. People wrongly assume that they could never lead a small group because they don't have a teaching gift.

- It takes a big slice of your meeting time, yet it can be the least interactive time. Relational conversations and contributions require *time*. (Arithmetically, if 12 people speak for 5 minutes that requires one hour!)

- There can be a subconscious devaluing of other aspects of group activity ("chat time is not as spiritual as teach time").

That said, there are times when teaching *is* required. For example, you may need to teach on discipleship and on community before embarking on this journey!

Facilitating practical conversations around living out what was taught on Sunday are often more helpful than traditional teaching. Such conversations give members a chance to ask questions and apply the message to their "real world".

As we strive to grow as disciples though, it can be helpful to take a different approach. Instead of teaching, or discussing the teaching, ask two "big questions" instead:

1. "What has Jesus said to you this week?" (A helpful sub-question is "how did you 'hear' that?")

2. "What have you done about it?" (A helpful sub-question is "how did it work out?")

This approach changes many group dynamics:

- The focus shifts away from the leader.

- The leader no longer carries the burden of teaching or being the primary contributor.

- The attention and burden shift to the group members; we want to know *their* answers to these questions! If we know that we will be

37

asked these questions, we are more likely to listen for Jesus' promptings and take steps of faith during the week!

- Anyone who is on a discipleship journey can contribute. You don't have to be a theologian, just an ordinary person who is listening for God speaking and acting on their conviction.

- Conversations move from "theory" or theology to "real-life discipleship" – the lives of your fellow disciples.

As you ask these questions, it is important to encourage people to:

- Tell "small stories" (like making a phone call because you felt prompted to), not just "big stories" (like healings and salvations).

- Tell stories of failure as well as success. (We learn a lot from our failures – and telling of our failures encourages everyone else who failed and didn't want to say so!)

Exploring your greater community

While each member has their individual "mission fields" (such as their workplaces and friendship circles), the group as a whole can also be a powerful influence in the greater community. The challenge is to recognise, and then take, the opportunities.

When all of the group members come from the same neighbourhood, this is their "greater community". For this reason, some prefer to establish, or even rearrange, their small groups in common geographic locations.

When the group members live further apart in different neighbourhoods, the "greater community" may be less obvious. It may be one neighbourhood – or it may be a community that the group recognise as one that they can impact together. Examples are a poor neighbourhood or shelter (visit, provide food parcels and other assistance), an old-age facility or hospital (visit regularly), or a school (form a "helping hands" group or a prayer group).

Some communities are not defined by geography, but by common life-stage or interest. Examples are parents of babies (so you could form a new parents' support group); participants in a sport (e.g. cycling, fishing, surfing or hiking); or enthusiasts of some sort (e.g. fans of live music or an art form).

You could even influence a community by meeting regularly at a local coffee shop (making your group visible to patrons and management).

Enjoy the adventure together!

Appendix: Five Levels of Communication

Level 1: Cliché Conversation

This type of talk is very safe. We use words such as "How are you?", "How's your family?", "Enjoying the rain?", or "I like your new hairstyle." In this type of conversation there is no personal sharing. Each person remains safely behind his or her "screen".

Level 2: Reporting the Facts about Others

In this kind of conversation we are content to tell others what someone else has said, but we offer no personal commentary on these facts. We just report the facts like the seven o'clock news each day. We share stories, but we do not commit ourselves as to how we feel about them.

Level 3: My Ideas and Judgments

This is where some real communication begins. We are willing to step out and risk telling some of our own ideas and decisions. We are probably still cautious however, and if we sense that what we are saying is not being accepted, we will retreat.

Level 4: My Feelings or Emotions

Now we share how we *feel* about facts, ideas and judgments. The feelings underneath these areas are revealed. If a person is to really share themselves with another individual, they must get to the level of sharing their feelings. Feelings should not be judged; they are our emotional state. Feelings are also subject to change; they express who we are at that moment.

Level 5: Completely Honest Communication of our Emotions and Personal Life

This is where we'd like to be in our community!

"Getting Real"

All deep relationships require openness and honesty. This may be difficult to achieve because it involves a risk – such as being rejected or dishonoured – but it is vital for relationships to grow. There will be times when this type of communication is achieved and other times when the communication is not as complete as it could be.

"There are two things, the actual and the ideal. To be mature is to see the ideal and live with the actual. To fail is to accept the actual and reject the ideal. To accept only that which is ideal and refuse the actual is to be immature. Do not criticize the actual because you have seen the ideal. Do not reject the ideal because you have seen the actual. Maturity is to live with the actual but hold on to the ideal."

- Derek Prince

Appendix: The Johari Window

The Johari Window is a simple and useful tool, designed to help us understand and improve in self-awareness, communications, relationships, group dynamics and community or team development. (It was developed by American psychologists Joseph Luft and Harry Ingham in the 1950's, calling it 'Johari' after combining their first names, Joe and Harry!)

		To myself:	
		Known to me	Unknown to me
To others:	Known to them	**open/free area** 'what we all know'	**blind area** 'what you don't tell me'
	Unknown to them	**hidden area** 'what I don't tell you'	**unknown area** 'what none of us see'

The open or free area: *what we all know*

This information is known by the person ('self') *and* by the group ('others'). This is the space where good communications and cooperation occur, free from misunderstanding.

The hidden area or 'façade': *what I don't tell you*

This is what is known to ourselves, but kept hidden from (and therefore unknown) to others. It is what we hide behind the "I'm doing fine" mask! It includes secrets, sensitivities, fears and hidden agendas.

The blind area or 'blind-spot': *what you don't tell me*

This is what is known *about* a person by others in the group, but is unknown by the person him/herself. It could also be referred to as 'ignorance about oneself'. (For example we may dominate conversations or have bad breath, but be unaware of it!)

Unknown area: *what none of us know*

Some things are unknown to a person and unknown to the others in the group.

Increasing the open area

We reduce the *hidden* area by *telling* the group the things that we have previously kept hidden. In order to do this, we need to feel secure; we cannot expect this of people until the community is healthy and the members recognize that this is a "safe place".

We reduce the *blind* area by *inviting* the group to speak into our lives. In order to do this, we need to feel loved by the group; we need to believe that they seek our highest good. As a group, we must learn to "speak the truth in love". When we point out something to a person that they seem unaware of, we do not criticize them. We do not break them down; we build them up.

www.ingramcontent.com/pod-product-compliance
Lightning Source LLC
Chambersburg PA
CBHW060544030426
42337CB00021B/4431